21st Century Skills Innovation Library

ANIMAL CROSSING:
Collecting Fish, Bugs, and Fossils

CHERRY LAKE PUBLISHING • ANN ARBOR, MICHIGAN

by Josh Gregory

CHERRY LAKE PRESS

Published in the United States of America by Cherry Lake Publishing
Ann Arbor, Michigan
www.cherrylakepublishing.com

Reading Adviser: Beth Walker Gambro, MS, Ed., Reading Consultant, Yorkville, IL

Cherry Lake Press is an imprint of Cherry Lake Publishing Group

Library of Congress Cataloging-in-Publication Data has been filed and is available
at catalog.loc.gov

Cherry Lake Publishing Group would like to acknowledge the work of the
Partnership for 21st Century Learning, a Network of Battelle for Kids. Please
visit http://www.batelleforkids.org/networks/p21 for more information.

Printed in the United States of America
Corporate Graphics

Contents

Chapter 1

On Display

If you've played *Animal Crossing: New Horizons*, you know that one of the best parts of the game is getting to explore your very own island. Every player's island is different, and you can customize yours to get it just the way you want it. But even though there's plenty of variety, some things are the same on

Exploring the great outdoors is a big part of having fun in *Animal Crossing: New Horizons*.

every player's island. One of them is that the game's **virtual** world is always packed with wildlife. The shadows of fish move back and forth lazily through the island's waterways and along the coast. Dragonflies dart through the air, and beetles cling to the sides of trees. No matter where you are on the island, you're bound to spot something moving around.

Early on in the game, you'll find out that the creatures living on your island aren't just for show. In fact, they are one of the main sources of activity in *Animal Crossing*. One of your main goals while playing will be to catch and catalog every wild **species** on the island. As you do, you will earn all kinds of rewards. You'll also get the satisfaction of filling in your Critterpedia. This is an app for your NookPhone that shows which animals you've caught so far. It also shows blank spaces for the ones you haven't caught yet. This means you can always see how close you are to catching everything.

When you first arrive on your island in *Animal Crossing*, there aren't many other characters there. One of the few who is around from the very beginning is Tom Nook. Tom will guide you through the many tasks needed to get a town up and running on the island. One thing he asks you to do early on is start catching fish and bugs. After you've caught five creatures, he will tell you about his friend Blathers. Blathers is a friendly owl who wants to set up a museum on the island. Tom will tell you to pick out a location for this museum, and Blathers will show up the next day.

Blathers

We accept donations of bugs, fish, and officially assessed fossils, as well as works of art...

You'll be talking to Blathers very often once you start collecting the local wildlife.

At first, Blathers will hang out in a tent. He needs to take care of a few things before he can set up a permanent museum building on the island. In the meantime, he asks you to start bringing him fish, bugs, or **fossils**. Once you have brought him 15 things, he will be ready to start construction on the museum. If you wait two days and come back, the museum will be ready to explore. From the outside, the museum looks about the same size as any other building in your town. But once you walk in the front door, you'll see that it's actually quite roomy.

Once the museum is built, you can always find Blathers near the entrance in the main room. Sometimes he will be napping or reading a book. He won't mind if you bother him, though. Talk to him anytime you want to donate something.

Head to the right from the museum entrance to reach the aquarium. Here, you'll see tanks filled with the different fish you've donated to Blathers so far. The aquarium is divided into two rooms. The one on the bottom is home to freshwater fish. These are the ones you can catch in rivers and ponds. The one on top holds creatures from the ocean. Near each fish tank, you'll see small information boards. Inspect these to get a close look at specific fish. This will also tell you the date you donated the fish to Blathers.

Bugs are displayed in the rooms to the left of the main museum entrance. There are three different rooms in this area. The first is a tree-filled **habitat** where different bugs can hang out in their natural environments. Like in the aquarium, you can inspect the signs to get a closer view of the bugs. There are also benches you can sit on to simply enjoy the peaceful view. Keep moving left from the first room and you will find yourself in the butterfly room. Here, colorful butterflies flap freely around a fountain. Head upward to reach the third room, where certain bug species are displayed in glass tanks.

The museum also has a large basement area you can reach by heading downstairs from the main entrance. Here, you'll find all the fossils you've donated so far. The first room contains fossils of ancient sea creatures. Keep going to find two rooms full of dinosaurs and other large animals. These exhibits are a lot of fun to explore. Follow the lines on the floors to see how these ancient species are related

In the Money

Capturing wildlife is more than just a way to fill up your museum exhibits. It's also one of the most reliable ways to make quick money in *Animal Crossing*. Once you bring Blathers a new species for the first time, he will no longer accept any more of that species. That means you can stockpile your duplicates and sell them to various shopkeepers around the island. Some of these creatures are very valuable. You might be surprised how fast you can make money by spending extra time fishing and bug hunting!

to each other and to the modern-day animal species on your island.

The museum is big to begin with, but it can get even bigger. After you've donated a total of 60 items to the museum, Blathers will mention that he'd like to set up an art exhibit. A new character called Redd will start visiting the island from time to time in his pirate ship. You can visit Redd to buy valuable works of art. Bring your first one to Blathers and he will get started adding a new section to the museum. Come back the next day and you'll find that there's now a huge second floor you can explore. Buy more art from Redd to fill up the displays here.

When you first explore the museum, its many rooms will mostly be empty. There's only one way to solve this problem: Get out there are start collecting!

Chapter 2

Hook, Line, and Sinker

Ready to start catching some fish? First, you'll need to find a fishing rod. You can purchase one from Timmy and Tommy. But it is much cheaper to simply **craft** one yourself. Very early in the game, Tom Nook will teach you how to craft items using DIY

You should try to carry a fishing rod wherever you go. You never know when you'll have the chance to catch a rare fish.

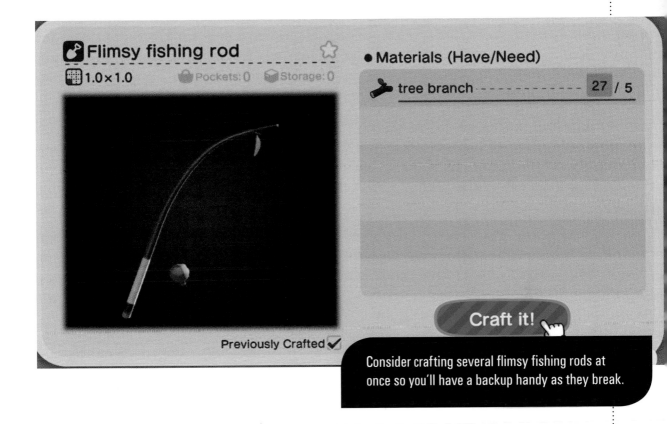

Consider crafting several flimsy fishing rods at once so you'll have a backup handy as they break.

(do-it-yourself) recipes. During this lesson, he will give you the recipe for a flimsy fishing rod. To craft it, all you need are five tree branches. Because these branches are common items around the island, you should always have the supplies for a fresh rod.

Like other tools in *Animal Crossing*, fishing rods will eventually break after you use them enough times. You can get different versions of these tools that will last for more uses. A flimsy fishing rod is the least **durable** rod in the game. It will break after about

7 to 10 uses. The improved version of this tool is simply called the fishing rod. To craft it, you'll need to purchase the item called Pretty Good Tools Recipes from Nook Stop in the Resident Services building. Once you have this, you can combine a flimsy fishing rod with an iron nugget to create a rod that lasts for 30 uses. Once you help them build the Nook's Cranny store and upgrade its size, Timmy and Tommy will

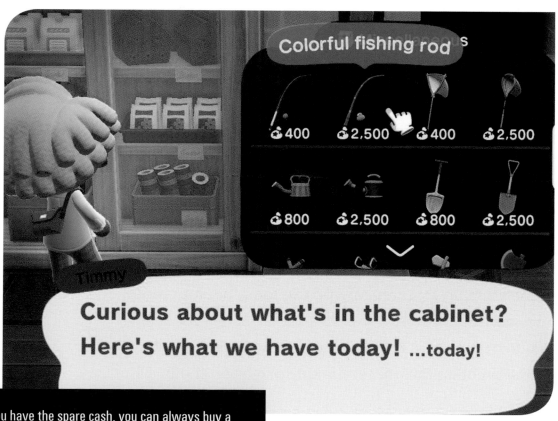

If you have the spare cash, you can always buy a fresh rod at Nook's Cranny.

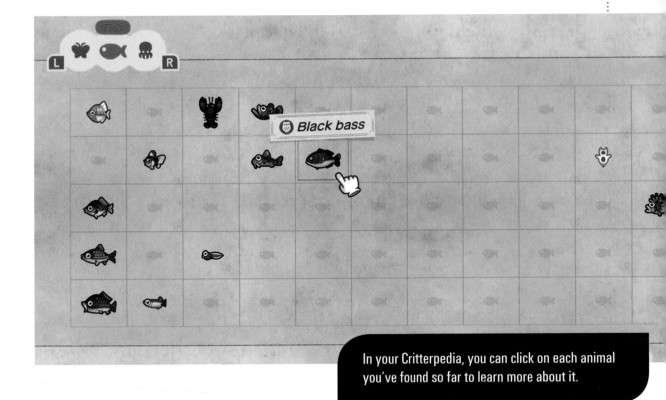

Black bass

In your Critterpedia, you can click on each animal you've found so far to learn more about it.

also sell special rods such as the colorful fishing rod, outdoorsy fishing rod, and fish fishing rod. These rods cannot be crafted. You have to purchase them from the store if you want to use them. Like the regular fishing rod, they will let you catch 30 fish before breaking. However, they have a different look.

There is one more fishing rod in the game. The golden fishing rod can only be crafted after you have completely filled in the fish section of your Critterpedia. As a reward for completing this tough task, the DIY recipe will soon arrive in your mailbox.

Something to Nibble On

When you are walking along the beach on your island, you might notice small jets of water spurting up from the sand. Use your shovel to dig at these spots and you'll usually get something called a manila clam. The first time you dig up a clam, you'll also get a new DIY recipe for fish bait! Dig up a few clams and take them to a workbench. Each clam can be crafted into a single piece of bait. Now take your bait to a body of water. Select it in your **inventory** and toss it into the water. Almost immediately, a fish will appear.

Bait really comes in handy when you are trying to get specific fish species. For example, if you know the fish you want can only be found in clifftop ponds, take a bunch of bait to the pond. Bait will always summon the type of fish that are in season and occur naturally in a location.

You'll need to use a rare gold nugget to craft the rod. It will be far more durable than any other fishing rod. However, it will still break eventually!

You need to have your fishing rod in your inventory to use it, so don't stash it in your house's storage. Equip a rod and head to any body of water. Now walk around until you see the shadow of a fish swimming. Don't hold the run button when you are near fish. If you do, they will swim away and you won't be able to catch them.

Note which direction the fish is facing and whether or not it is moving. Stand near the edge of the water and press the A button to cast your line. You want to aim your cast so it lands in front of the fish. It should be close enough for the fish to see, but not right on top of the fish. It will probably take you a few tries to get used to aiming your cast. Once you get the hang of it, it will be like second nature.

Your bobber will float in the water at the spot you casted to. The fish should notice and swim toward your bobber. It might nibble at your line a couple of times before taking the bait. Be patient. If you try to reel it in

Sometimes you'll reel in trash instead of a fish. You can sell these items or use them in certain crafting recipes.

too soon, the fish will get away. As soon as your bobber goes completely underwater, press and hold the A button. If you timed it right, your character will reel the fish onto land and let you know which species it is. Congratulations! You've caught your first fish.

There are 80 different fish to catch in *Animal Crossing: New Horizons*. That might not seem like a lot at first. After all, it only takes a few seconds to catch a fish. However, each species only shows up under certain conditions and in certain places. You can't simply go out and catch them all at once. It will take a lot of patience and a little luck to fill in the fish section of

The butterfly display is one of the most scenic parts of Blathers's museum.

your Critterpedia. However, there are a few tricks you can learn to help you determine the right time and place to catch the ones you still need.

Just like in real life, some *Animal Crossing* fish can only be found in certain kinds of waterways. Some only swim in the river that snakes its way across your island. Some only live in ponds, and some can only be caught in the sea by fishing on the beach or from a dock. You also need to consider **elevation** for some species. There are fish that can only be caught atop the highest cliffs on the island. There are also some that only swim in the area where the river meets the sea.

Some fish can only be caught at certain times of year. The available fish change each month. Some are almost always in season, while others only give you a short window of time to catch them each year. The months each fish is available stay the same each year, though. This means you can try again next year if you miss it the first time. Certain species are also only active at night or during the day. There is even one fish that can only be caught when it is raining.

You can't tell exactly what fish is swimming in the water before you catch it. However, you can get a clue based on the size of its shadow. There are six different shadow sizes, from a tiny one to a very big one. You can use this information to help you track down specific species. For example, if you know you are looking for a fish that swims in rivers and has the largest shadow, you can ignore the shadows that don't match this description.

From time to time, a character named C.J. will visit your island. This friendly beaver is a fishing fanatic. He will pay more for fish than Timmy and Tommy. If you've got a bunch of duplicate fish you don't need, be sure to sell them when C.J. comes around. C.J. can also make statues of different fish. To get these, you'll need three of the same fish. You'll also have to give C.J. a different amount of Bells depending on which fish you want to use. C.J. will take your fish and your money and mail you a statue the next day.

C.J. is also the host of special Fishing Tourney events on your island. Fishing Tourneys are held four times each year. Keep an eye on the notice board in the center of town to see when one is coming up. To participate, talk to C.J. during a Tourney. You will then get 3 minutes to catch as many fish as you can. Your rod will not break during this time, and the size of the fish doesn't matter. It's all about catching as many as you can during the time limit. You'll earn points that can be exchanged for trophies and other prizes.

There are also some sea creatures that swim too deep to be caught with a fishing rod. These sea creatures have their own tab in the Critterpedia. There are 40 of them, and you'll need a wetsuit to start catching them. Simply purchase one from Nook's Cranny and you'll be ready to get started.

Put on the wetsuit from your inventory screen. Then walk up to the edge of the water along the beach and press the A button to go swimming. While swimming, look for bubbles that rise up from the water. These show where a sea creature is located. Swim to the bubbles and press the Y button to dive down. For some creatures, this is all you need to do. You will automatically capture the creature. Other times, the creature will move away from you. Tap the A button while you are underwater and hold the left stick in the direction you want to swim. When you bump into the creature you will capture it. Just like regular fish, different sea creatures are only available in certain months or at certain times of day.

Chapter 3

Creepy Crawlers

J ust like you need a fishing rod to start catching fish, you'll need a net to begin bug hunting. You can get a net the same ways you get a fishing rod. Either buy one from Timmy and Tommy or craft one on your own. If you want to upgrade from the flimsy net to the regular net, you'll need the Pretty Good Tools Recipes from Nook Stop. And if you want the amazing gold net, you'll need to catch every bug in the

I caught a damselfly!
Now it's a damselfly in distress!

The game will make a little joke about the name of each bug you catch.

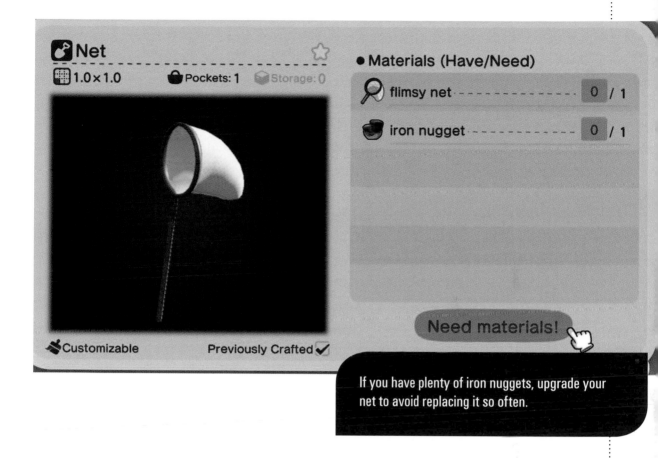

☉ Net	☆
1.0 × 1.0 Pockets: 1 Storage: 0	

● Materials (Have/Need)

🔍 flimsy net	0 / 1
🥫 iron nugget	0 / 1

Customizable   Previously Crafted ✓

Need materials! 🖐

If you have plenty of iron nuggets, upgrade your net to avoid replacing it so often.

Critterpedia. Finally, Nook Stop will eventually start selling colorful nets, star nets, and outdoorsy nets. These can't be crafted and don't offer any special benefits. They simply look different from regular nets.

In some ways, catching bugs is a lot simpler than fishing. All you need to do is equip your net and get near a bug. Then press the A button to swing your net and capture the creature. But there are also some unique challenges to face if you want to collect all 80 bug species.

Unlike fish, you can see exactly what bug species you are hunting before you catch it. The catch is that each bug moves and reacts to you in different ways. Some simply fly around. Others crawl on the ground or live in trees. Some only show up during very specific conditions. There are even bugs that will attack if you startle them. Wasps will chase you down and sting you if you accidentally knock their nests out of trees. The first time they sting, your character's eye will be swollen. You'll need to take some medicine to fix it. If you get stung a second time before taking

A sting will leave your villager with a swollen eye until you use medicine to heal it.

Sneak up very carefully on bugs that perch atop flowers. Otherwise they might fly away before you can swipe them!

medicine, your character will faint and wake up at home. Tarantulas and scorpions will also attack if you move toward them while their legs are raised. To approach one, only move when the creature puts its legs down. Otherwise it will bite. A single bite causes your character to faint right away.

You'll need to sneak up on certain kinds of bugs. Hold down the A button when your net is equipped. Your character will raise the net and begin walking very slowly. Let go of the button when you get close to the bug and your character will swing the net quickly.

Bugs can also hide in unseen locations. Many will stay in treetops unless you shake the tree to knock them loose. Others hide under rocks. Try banging a rock with your shovel and something might just come scuttling out from underneath.

Just like fish, some bugs are only available during certain months or times of day. Others only come out when it is raining or can only be found in certain areas of the island. And some bugs only show up on your island in very specific situations. For example, there are bugs that only come around when you have flowers that are a certain color. This is more complicated than it might seem. To get some flower colors, you'll have to spend time **breeding** flowers. Other bugs only show up around rotten fruit, or when you cut down trees and leave the stumps in place.

A red lizard named Flick will occasionally visit your island. Flick is a lot like C.J., but he is interested in bugs instead of fish. He will pay extra for any bugs you want to sell. He can also make bug statues for you if you give him bugs and Bells. He also hosts special events called Bug Offs. A Bug Off is just like a Fishing Tourney, but for bugs. You'll have 3 minutes to catch

Hunting Trips

Looking for fish and bugs that don't seem to show up on your island? Try using Nook Miles to purchase a ticket to a mystery island. These islands are packed with plants, animals, and other useful collectibles. You can also try visiting a friend's island. They might have bugs you haven't seen on your island yet. Of course, you can also trade with a friend who has the things you're looking for. Be sure to offer something good in return!

as many bugs as you can. Your net won't break during this time, and you can earn points to exchange for valuable prizes.

Chapter 4

Digging Deep

Collecting fossils is much simpler than capturing living animals. To get started, you'll need a shovel. You can't get this handy tool until Blathers comes to your island. One of the first things he will do is give you DIY recipes for a vaulting pole and a flimsy shovel. You'll need the pole to reach the areas of your island beyond the river. And of course, you'll need the shovel to dig.

There are parts of the island that you won't be able to reach at first without a vaulting pole.

Look! I dug up
a fossil!

It's worth tracking down all of the fossils on your island each day you play.

Just like the fishing rod and the net, the flimsy shovel can be upgraded to regular and golden versions once you have the necessary DIY recipes. There are also three special shovels that can only be purchased from Nook's Cranny.

Once you have a shovel, wander the island in search of dark, star-shaped spots on the ground. Use your shovel to dig on these spots. Sometimes you might find items or even just an empty hole. But most often, you will find a fossil. A few fossils will appear on your island each day. If you think you found them all, come back the next day to find more.

At first, you won't know what fossil you found. Bring it to Blathers and ask him to assess it. He will tell you what the fossil is and let you know if you've donated one to the museum yet. Some fossils are complete all on their own. Others are pieces of larger

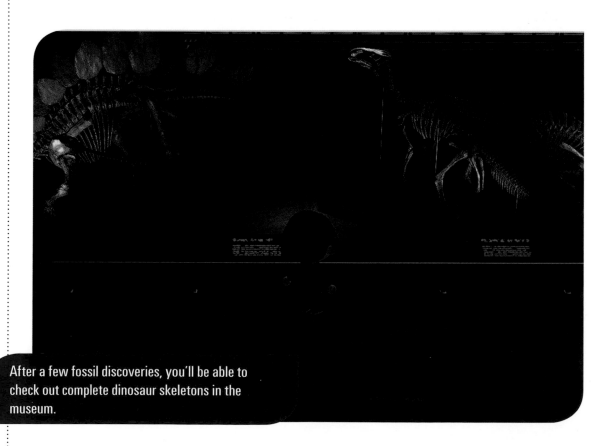

After a few fossil discoveries, you'll be able to check out complete dinosaur skeletons in the museum.

Showing Off

The museum isn't the only place you can put your discoveries on display. If you have a fish, bug, or fossil in your inventory, try dropping it on the ground. It will pop up and act just like a decoration or piece of furniture. You can push, pull, and rotate it to get it exactly where you want it. Fish and bugs will be inside glass boxes, while fossils will be displayed on stands. These can be a great way to decorate your home or liven up the island.

creatures. For example, you'll need six different fossils to complete the diplodocus skeleton in the museum.

That's all there is to it. Simply try to find as many fossils as you can each day. It will take a little luck to get them all. Don't forget that you can trade with friends, though. This is often the best way to get what you need once your museum is mostly full. Fossils are also worth a good amount of money, so they are always worth digging up, even if you already have them all.

As you collect more and more items, your museum will really come to life. Visit frequently to check out what's on display. The next time your friends visit your island, they'll be impressed to see everything you've found!

Glossary

breeding (BREE-ding) intentionally mating plants together to produce new plants with certain features

craft (KRAFT) make or build something

durable (DUR-uh-buhl) tough and long-lasting

elevation (el-uh-VAY-shuhn) a measurement of how high something is above sea level

fossils (FAH-suhlz) the preserved remains of living things from the distant past

habitat (HAB-uh-tat) the type of place where a type of living thing naturally lives

inventory (IN-vuhn-toh-ree) a list of the items your character is carrying in a video game

species (SPEE-sheez) a particular category of animals or other living things

virtual (VUR-choo-uhl) existing in a computer program, but not in real life

Find Out More

BOOKS

Cunningham, Kevin. *Video Game Designer*. Ann Arbor, MI: Cherry Lake Publishing, 2016.

Loh-Hagan, Virginia. *Video Games*. Ann Arbor, MI: Cherry Lake Publishing, 2021.

Powell, Marie. *Asking Questions About Video Games*. Ann Arbor, MI: Cherry Lake Publishing, 2016.

WEBSITES

Animal Crossing Wiki

https://animalcrossing.fandom.com/wiki/Animal_Crossing: _New_Horizons
This fan-created site is packed with info about every detail of the *Animal Crossing* games.

Island News — *Animal Crossing: New Horizons*

https://www.animal-crossing.com/new-horizons/news
Keep up to date with the latest official news updates about *Animal Crossing*.

Index

About the Author

Josh Gregory is the author of more than 150 books for kids. He has written about everything from animals to technology to history. A graduate of the University of Missouri–Columbia, he currently lives in Chicago, Illinois.